T0277319

Neuro Navigation Publishing
777 N. Jefferson Street
Milwaukee, WI 53202

Introduction

This is the second book in a series about Kelly's experiences. Kelly is a neurodivergent learner in a neurotypical school. She shows the challenges and triumphs of her journey to succeed at school and make friends. She also learns about her specific learning disabilities. This book uses dyslexia friendly font.

Specific Learning Disabilities

Receiving   Processing

Communicating   Recalling

Math

Reading

Writing

Spelling

Auditory processing

Sensory / motor

Emotional

Social

Specific learning disabilities:

Dyscalculia:
Challenge to understand and solve math problems.

Dyslexia:
Difficult to read, write, and spell words.

Dyspraxia:
Difficult to coordinate muscles, and balancing.

Dysgraphia:
Struggle to write legibly and coherently.

Kelly goes to Perry Elementary School.

Miss Parker teaches math.

All the other students understand, but Kelly.

Kelly and her mom meet with Dr. Julie Smith, PhD.

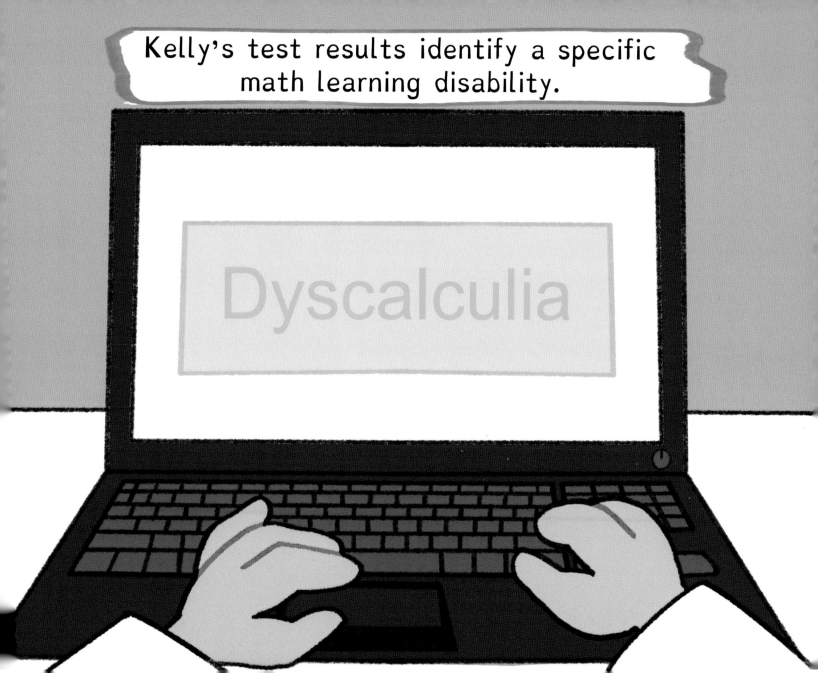

"We have an answer! Her test results revealed she has dyscalculia," Dr. Smith told Kelly and her mom.

Kelly's mom tells Miss Parker, "Dr. Smith said Kelly has dyscalculia. This means she learns math differently."

Kelly's mom continues to say to Miss Parker, "Kelly needs these tools and resources to help her learn math."

Fun questions about Clever Girl!

1. How many books are stacked on Dr. Smith's desk?

2. Can you name the math signs on Miss Parker's shirt?

3. How many windows can you see on Perry Elementary building?

4. How many times do you see Louis the cat?

5. After 90, what should the next skip number be on the math classroom wall?

6. How many students are in Kelly's math classroom?

7. Can you count the number of kids who have brown eyes?

8. If there are nine students, how many total eyes do you count?

If you're having trouble in school tell someone and get help!
www.Neuro-Navigation.com

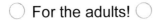 For the adults!

List of Kelly's math accommodations

Provide charts of math facts or multiplication tables

Create separate worksheet for word problems

Use of a calculator when computation is not being assessed

Use visual and kinesthetic techniques when teaching concepts

Allow extra time for assignments

Why should you read Kelly's book: "The Child Who Learned Differently"

The Child Who Learned Differently

Parents and caregivers of neurodivergent learners will gain a better understanding of the challenges faced by neurodivergent children and discover strategies to support them.

Educators and school administrators will read the book to gain insights to create an inclusive learning environment for neurodivergent learners.

Neurodivergent learners will relate to this book, feel less alone, find inspiration, discover strategies, and courage for self-advocacy to succeed.

Organization leaders who have neurodivergent learners on their workforce will have insight for reviewing their procedures to find a inclusive work environment for all.